THE CONVERSATION TRAIN

of related interest

What Did You Say? What Do You Mean?
120 Illustrated Metaphor Cards, plus Booklet
with Information, Ideas and Instructions
Jude Welton
Illustrated by Jane Telford
ISBN 978 1 84310 924 2

It's Raining Cats and Dogs
An Autism Spectrum Guide to the Confusing World
of Idioms, Metaphors and Everyday Expressions
Michael Barton
ISBN 978 1 84905 283 2
eISBN 978 0 85700 588 5

The One and Only Sam
A Story Explaining Idioms for Children with Asperger
Syndrome and Other Communication Difficulties
Aileen Stalker
Illustrated by Bob Spencer
ISBN 978 1 84905 040 1
eISBN 978 0 85700 214 3

Kevin Thinks
...about Outer Space, Confusing Expressions and the
Perfectly Logical World of Asperger Syndrome
Gail Watts
ISBN 978 1 84905 292 4
eISBN 978 0 85700 615 8

THE CONVERSATION TRAIN

A VISUAL APPROACH TO CONVERSATION FOR CHILDREN ON THE AUTISM SPECTRUM

JOEL SHAUL, LCSW

Jessica Kingsley *Publishers*
London and Philadelphia

This edition published in 2014
by Jessica Kingsley Publishers
73 Collier Street
London N1 9BE, UK
and
400 Market Street, Suite 400
Philadelphia, PA 19106, USA

www.jkp.com

Copyright © Joel Shaul 2010 and 2014
First published in 2010 by Autism Teaching Strategies

Library of Congress Cataloging in Publication Data
A CIP catalog record for this book is available from the Library of Congress

British Library Cataloguing in Publication Data
A CIP catalogue record for this book is available from the British Library

ISBN 978 1 84905 986 2
eISBN 978 0 85700 900 5

Printed and bound in China

2/13/15 OCLC

CONTENTS

Introduction

Many children, especially children with autism spectrum disorders (ASDs), are fascinated by trains.

Children with ASDs often struggle with basic conventions of conversation, such as greetings, goodbyes, adherence to a shared interest, and tactful shifting of topics. I created *The Conversation Train to* help children with ASDs learn some aspects of conversation that happen to correspond with railroads.

Trains and railroads provide convenient metaphors for many elements of conversation: locomotives are like greetings; they get the train going. Train cars are like conversation turns; it is good to have at least a few when you are in a conversation. A switch track changes a train from one track to another, just like two people switching to a new topic. A conversation that gets "derailed" is like a derailed train. A caboose ends the train (at least in the olden days); people need to end their conversations the right way and say goodbye.

PROMOTE SKILL GENERALIZATION USING THE TRAIN IMAGERY

Many of the words we use to teach children the pragmatics of speech tend to be rather blunt, and some other words can be unclear in their meaning. Some examples of harsh and confusing comments are "That's off topic" and "You've been going on too long." Most children grasp the basics of *The Conversation Train* fairly quickly. Once children master the concepts and language, you may consider referring to the train when coaching children in conversation. For example:

"Remember the locomotive."

"Let's get it back on the track."

"Let's make the train longer."

"Maybe the train is long enough."

"Remember the caboose."

USING THE WORKSHEETS

The worksheets provide helpful extension activities to use with *The Conversation Train*. The worksheets in Section Two are designed to be used repeatedly and can be photocopied. It is particularly important to have the child complete The Two-Person, On-Track Worksheet with multiple individuals, to reinforce the understanding that "on-track" topics are different between one conversation partner and the next.

SECTION ONE

THE CONVERSATION TRAIN

When people talk together, it is like a train.

PART ONE

STARTING A CONVERSATION

The locomotive starts the train.

Without a locomotive,
it's hard to start a train.

"Hello."

"Hi."

"Good morning."

Without words like these, it's
hard to start a conversation.

The coal car, or "tender," comes next.

The coal gives the train power.

"How are you?"

"How's it going?"

"What's up?"

These words give the conversation power, just as coal gives power to the train.

These words help move the conversation forward.

"Hello."

"Hi."

"How are you?"

"Good, thanks."

PART TWO
TAKING TURNS IN CONVERSATION

This is a train car.

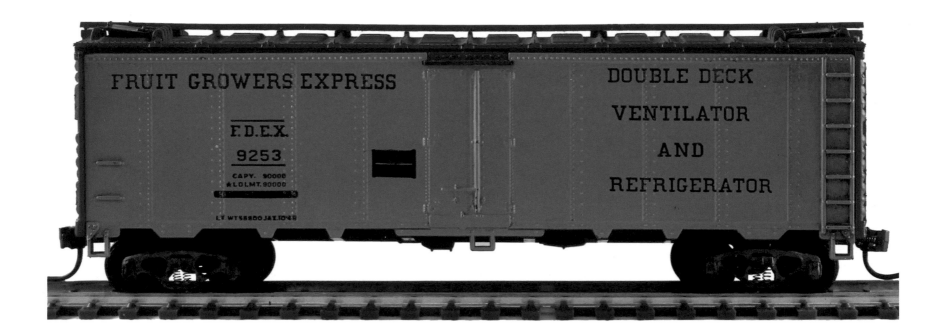

Every train should have at least a few of these.

Each train car is like a *conversation turn*.

A conversation turn happens each time people talk back and forth in a conversation.

Conversation is more than two people just saying words. One person talks about what the other person has just said.

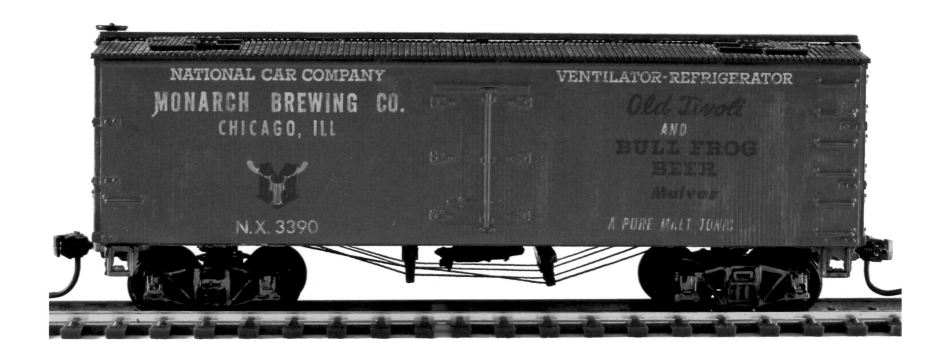

"So, how do you like this snow we've been getting?"

"Great! We had a snowball fight last night!"

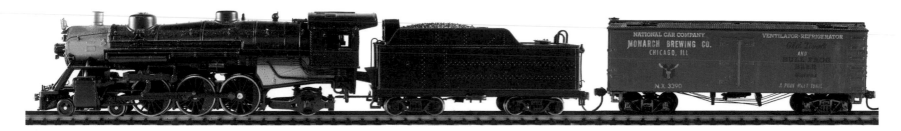

"Hi."

"Hello."

"How are you?"

"Fine, thanks."

"So, how do you like this snow we've been getting?"

"Great! We had a snowball fight last night!"

PART THREE

STAYING ON TRACK

A train needs to stay on the track.

Conversations have to stay on track too.

"Hi."

"Hello."

"How are you?"

"Fine, thanks."

"So, how do you like this snow we've been getting?"

"Great! We had a snowball fight last night!"

"I heard it might snow again."

"I hope so. I want to miss school again."

OFF TRACK

"Hi."

"Hello."

"How are you?"

"Fine, thanks."

"So, how do you like this snow we've been getting?"

"Great! We had a snowball fight last night!"

"I heard it might snow again."

"I got a new Pokémon card!"

If you go off track too often, people might get tired of talking to you.

They might find someone else to talk to.

Read this conversation out loud with the adult who is with you now.

Figure out something "on track" to say at the end.

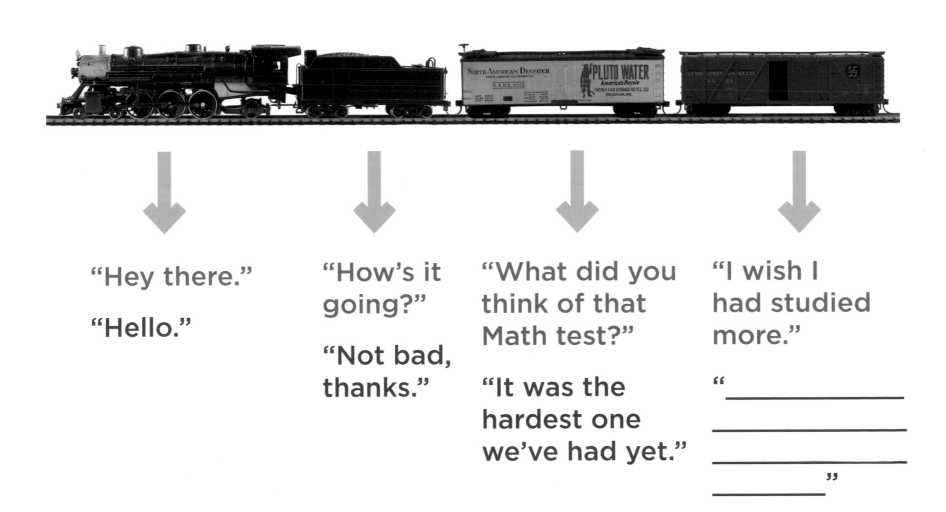

"Hey there."

"Hello."

"How's it going?"

"Not bad, thanks."

"What did you think of that Math test?"

"It was the hardest one we've had yet."

"I wish I had studied more."

"_____
_____
_____
_____"

Now try this one.

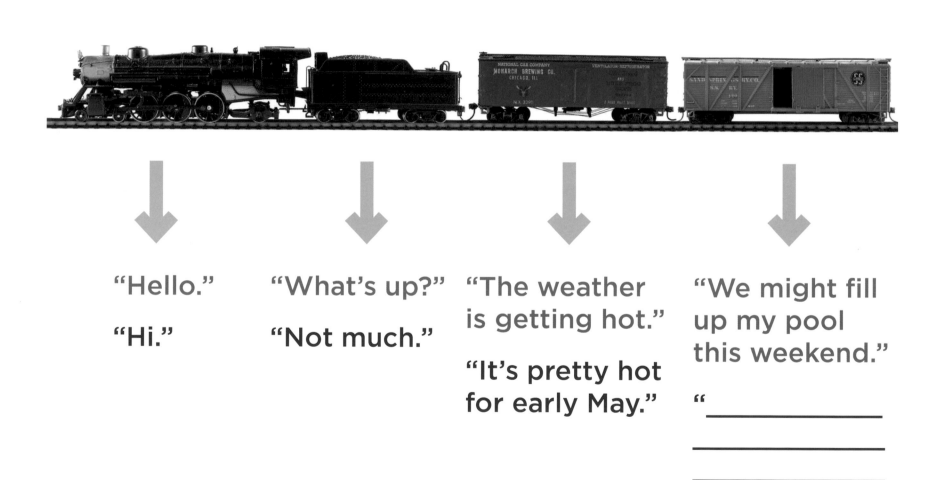

"Hello."

"Hi."

"What's up?"

"Not much."

"The weather is getting hot."

"It's pretty hot for early May."

"We might fill up my pool this weekend."

"_____

_____

_____

_____,"

Try another.

For this one, you need to say something "on track" in two places.

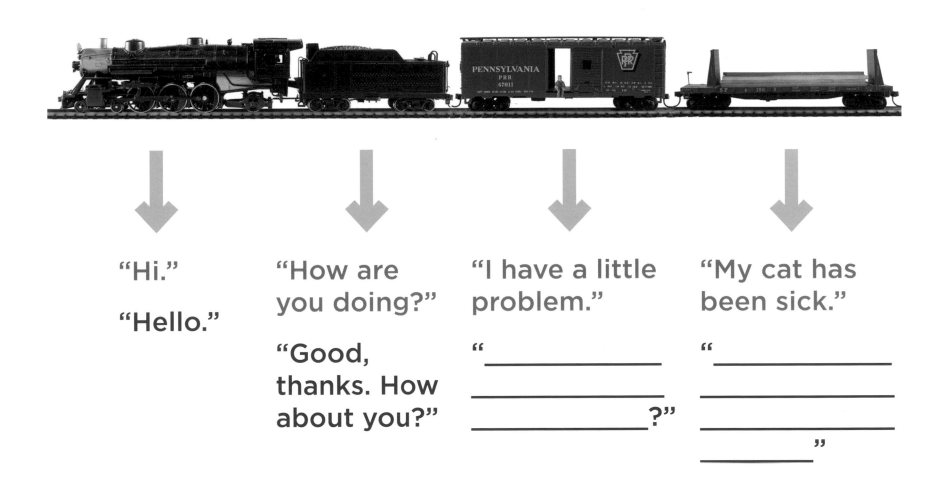

"Hi."

"Hello."

"How are
you doing?"

"Good,
thanks. How
about you?"

"I have a little
problem."

"_____

_____

_____?"

"My cat has
been sick."

"_____

_____

_____

_____"

Have a conversation with someone now.

Keep it on track, and point to a train car for each
conversation turn back and forth until you reach the end.

Here's a longer one. Stay on track with
the other person, all the way to the end.

PART FOUR

CHANGING TOPICS

When people talk, sometimes they may
want to stay on the same topic.

Here is an example of staying on the same topic.

People talking
together can
decide to switch
to a new topic.

When people want the new topic, they go on a new "track."

Don't go *off track* when switching topics.

Here, one person tries to force a new topic the other person does not care about.

By talking on and on about dragons, one person
is going off on a new track, all alone.

PART FIVE

ENDING THE CONVERSATION

Some conversations are very short.

Some conversations are very long.

39

All conversations, short or long, must come to an end.

You should end the conversation the right way.
Don't just stop talking or walk away.

Finishing the conversation has two parts.

First part:

"I've got to go now."

"Time for class."

"My ride is here."

"My dad is calling me for dinner."

Second part

"Goodbye."

"See you later."

"Goodnight."

"So long."

PART SIX

PUTTING IT ALL TOGETHER

"Hello."

"Hi."

"Good morning."

"How are you?"

"How's it going?"

Talk back and forth in conversation turns.

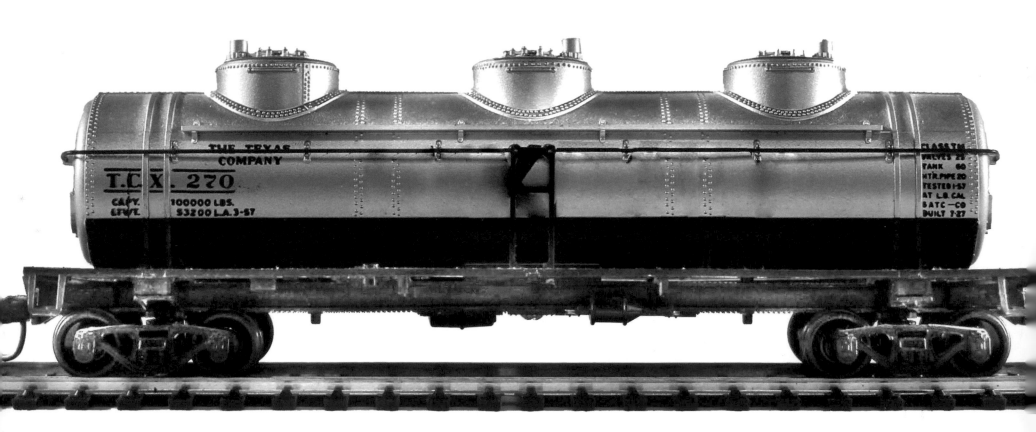

Stay on topics you and the other person both want.

Finish the conversation the right way.

THE END

SECTION TWO

THE CONVERSATION TRAIN WORKSHEETS

WHAT DO THE DIFFERENT PARTS OF THE TRAIN MEAN?

Name _____

Draw a line connecting each train part with the different parts of a conversation.

"Hello."
"Hi."
"Good morning."

A conversation turn: two people talking back and forth one time

Ending the conversation the right way

One person switching to a topic the other person does not want

Both people start talking about something else

"How are you?"
"How's it going?"

HELLO WORDS, HOW ARE YOU WORDS, SWITCH TRACK WORDS AND GOODBYE WORDS

Name _____

Connect the words and groups of words with the locomotive, coal tender, switch track and caboose.
There can be more than one answer for some of them. (We did one for you.)

"How have you been?"		"See you tomorrow."
"It's been nice talking to you."		"How's it going?"
"Good morning."		"Hello."
"By the way…"		"That reminds me of something else."
"Speaking of…"		"Hi."
"How are you?"		"What have you been up to lately?"
"Goodnight."		"I guess I ought to say bye now."
"Well, I have to go now."		

Fix the Mixed-Up Conversation

Name _____

This conversation is all mixed up. Can you put it in the right order? Draw lines connecting the bits of conversation with the correct parts of the train. (We did one for you.)

"Hey, what did you think of that test we just had?"
"It's the hardest one we have had so far."

"Well, the teacher is calling us. See you later."
"Yeah, see you later, Mike."

"Hello, Mike."
"Hi, Holly."

"I agree. The first test last week was easier."
"Yeah. I had no problem with that first test."

"How are you today?"
"Good, thanks."

"By the way, I noticed you're wearing green like me."
"Happy St. Patrick's Day. Your green socks are cool."

"Last night they started the new season of SpongeBob."
"Mike, you know I don't watch SpongeBob."

THINGS YOU LOVE CAN MAKE YOU GO OFF TRACK

Name _____

Often, people go "off track" by talking too much about the things they love.
What are some things that *you* love a lot...
...but that *other people* might not like to talk about as much as you do?

**Your favorite
video game**

**Your favorite toy
to play with**

_____

_____

**Your favorite TV
show or movie**

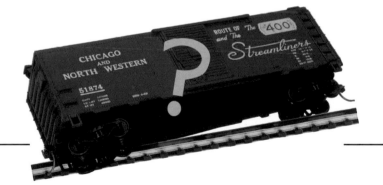

**Another
favorite thing**

_____

_____

**Your favorite
YouTube video**

**Another
favorite thing**

_____

_____

✓

People you know and what they like talking about

Name _____

Other people have their own minds and their own things they like talking about.
Think about some people you know. Write down what each person likes talking about.

1
Somebody in my home named
_____

This person likes doing
_____

This person likes eating
_____

This person likes watching
_____

This person likes playing
_____

2
Somebody in my home named
_____

This person likes doing
_____

This person likes eating
_____

This person likes watching
_____

This person likes playing
_____

3
Somebody in my school named
_____

This person likes doing
_____

This person likes eating
_____

This person likes watching
_____

This person likes playing
_____

4
Somebody in my school named
_____

This person likes doing
_____

This person likes eating
_____

This person likes watching
_____

This person likes playing
_____

PEOPLE YOU KNOW AND WHAT YOU BOTH LIKE TALKING ABOUT

Name _____

What is something you and this other person *both* like talking about?
What does this person *not* like talking about? Write down your answers.

1

Somebody in my home named

_____

We both like talking about

_____

With this person, I should avoid talking too much about

_____

2

Somebody in my home named

_____

We both like talking about

_____

With this person, I should avoid talking too much about

_____

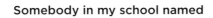

3

Somebody in my school named

_____

We both like talking about

_____

With this person, I should avoid talking too much about

_____

4

Somebody in my school named

_____

We both like talking about

_____

With this person, I should avoid talking too much about

_____

THE TWO-PERSON, ON-TRACK WORKSHEET

Name _____

1 Two people fill this worksheet out together at the same time by writing their interests on either side.

2 They write in the middle the things they both like.

3 They talk about these things together.

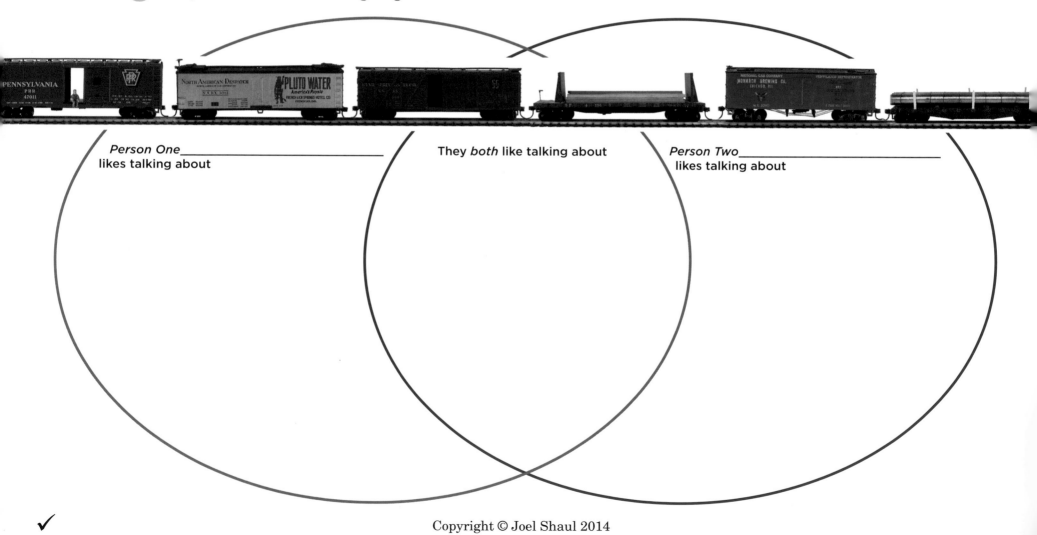

Person One_____
likes talking about

They *both* like talking about

Person Two_____
likes talking about

CHOOSING THE RIGHT WORDS WITH DIFFERENT PEOPLE

Name _____

With different people, you need to choose whether to be more or less *serious* or *formal*.

A	B	C
Very relaxed (informal)	**More serious (formal)**	**Very formal**

"Hi there."	"Hi."	"Hello."
"Howdy."	"Good morning."	
"Hey."		

"Yo, dude."	"How are you doing?"	"How do you do?"
"What's up?"	"How have you been?"	"How are you?"
"What's going on?"		

"How's it going?"	"Goodbye."	"Farewell."
"Catch you later."	"Goodnight."	"Goodbye."
"See you later."	"I'll see you later."	"Goodnight."
"I'm out of here!"	"I'll see you tomorrow."	
"So long!"		

When you are saying "Hello," "How are you?" and "Goodbye" to these different people, which would you pick: A, B, or C?

Circle your answer.

1. Meeting your new principal or headmaster   A   B   C

2. Seeing your friend on the playground   A   B   C

3. Meeting your adult neighbor for the first time   A   B   C

4. Saying goodbye to someone on your team   A   B   C

5. Meeting your mother's boss   A   B   C

6. Seeing the man who cuts your dad's hair   A   B   C

7. Saying goodbye to a kid you met at a birthday party   A   B   C

KEEPING TRACK OF STAYING ON TRACK

Name _____

Write about some different times you spoke with people.

1

I talked on track with _____

I started the conversation by saying

_____

_____

We talked about _____

_____

_____

I finished the conversation by saying

_____

_____

2

I talked on track with _____

I started the conversation by saying

_____

_____

We talked about _____

_____

_____

I finished the conversation by saying

_____

_____

✓

Conversation Train Coloring Pages

Name _____

Color in these pictures.

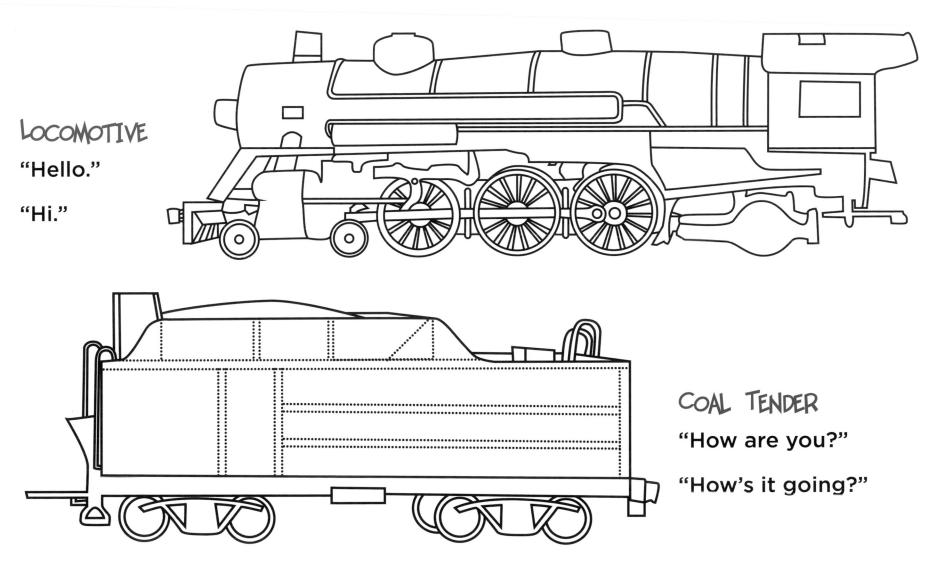

Locomotive

"Hello."

"Hi."

Coal Tender

"How are you?"

"How's it going?"

Name _____

TRAIN CAR

Two people
talking back
and forth.

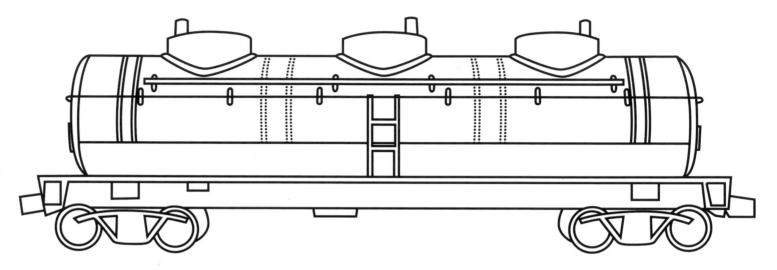

TRAIN CAR

Two people
talking back
and forth.

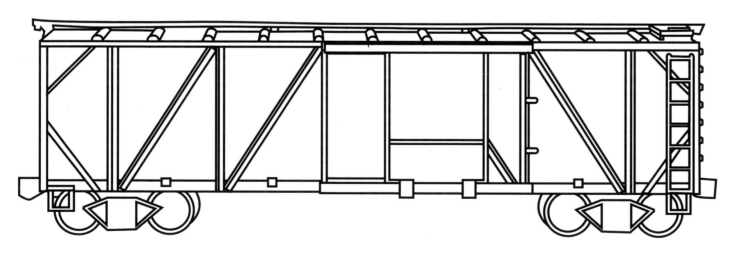

✓

Name _____

OFF-TRACK CAR

Someone suddenly switching the topic to something the other person does not want.

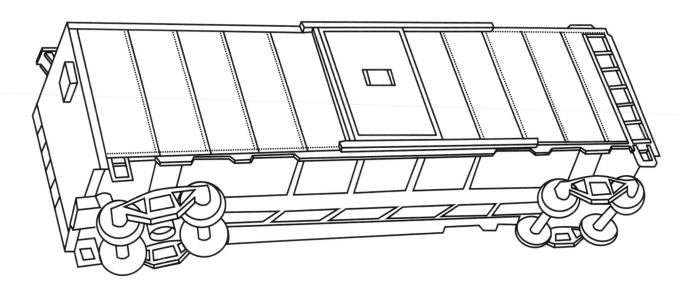

CABOOSE

Ending the conversation the right way.

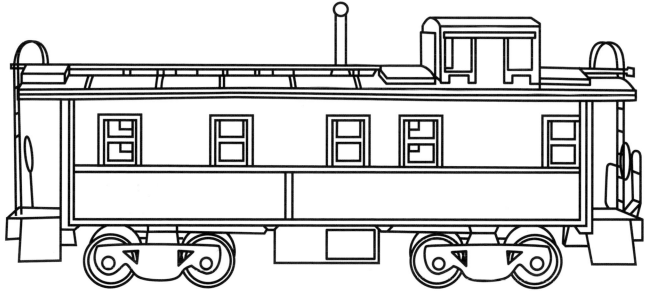

✓